Astrology can be used as a map that helps you see the road ahead. The position of the stars and planets at the exact time you were born influence your personality and life path. It can help you understand yourself and others better by showing you patterns and characteristics associated with each zodiac sign. To learn astrology you must start with the basics...the zodiac signs.

WHY I'M ME

MY NAME: _____

MY DATE OF BIRTH: _____

MY TIME OF BIRTH: _____

MY CITY/STATE OF BIRTH: _____

MY SUN SIGN: _____

MY RISING/ASCENDANT SIGN: _____

MY MOON SIGN: _____

MY MERCURY SIGN: _____

MY MARS SIGN: _____

MY VENUS SIGN: _____

FREE BIRTH CHARTS ARE AVAILABLE ONLINE

USE YOUR FREE BIRTH CHART TO FILL IN YOUR WHEEL

ADD THE 12 ZODICAC SIGNS FROM YOUR BIRTH CHART

FOUR ELEMENTS OF THE ZODIAC SIGNS

FIRE, EARTH, AIR, WATER

ELEMENT TRIGONS

 FIRE TRIGON: ARIES, LEO, SAGITTARIUS

 EARTH TRIGON: TAURUS, VIRGO, CAPRICORN

AIR TRIGON: GEMINI, LIBRA, AQUARIUS

 WATER TRIGON: CANCER, SCORPIO, PISCES

MY ELEMENT

MY ELEMENT: _____

MY TRIGON: _____

PEOPLE WHO ARE IN MY TRIGON: _____

_____

_____

HOW ARE WE ALIKE: _____

_____

_____

THREE MODALITIES OF THE ZODIAC SIGNS

HOW THE ZODIAC SIGNS EXPRESS THEIR ENERGY

FIXED: TAURUS, LEO, SCORPIO, AQUARIUS
FIXED SIGNS ARE KNOWN FOR THEIR STABILITY AND
ENDURANCE. THEY ARE PERSISTENT AND CAN SEE THINGS
THROUGH UNTIL THE END.

CARDINAL: ARIES, CANCER, LIBRA, CAPRICORN
CARDINAL SIGNS ARE THE INITIATORS. THEY TAKE ACTION.
THEY MAKE GOOD LEADERS AND THEY ARE DECISIVE.

MUTABLE: GEMINI, VIRGO, SAGITTARIUS, PISCES
MUTABLE SIGNS ARE THE ADAPTORS. THEY ARE FLEXIBLE &
ABLE TO CHANGE WITH CIRCUMSTANCES. THEY ARE
VERSATILE AND CAN SEE MULTIPLE SIDES TO ANY
SITUATION.

MY MODALITY

MY MODALITY: _____

MY ENERGY IS: _____

PEOPLE WHO SHARE MY MODALITY: _____

_____

_____

HOW ARE WE ALIKE: _____

_____

_____

FIRE SIGNS

ARIES, LEO, SAGITTARIUS

People born under the fire element are often full of energy and enthusiasm. They are like a warm, glowing flame that can inspire others. Fire signs are confident and passionate, but they can also be quick-tempered and impulsive.

MY FIRE SIGNS

MY FIRE SIGNS: _____

FIRE SIGNS I KNOW: _____

HOW ARE WE ALIKE: _____

_____

_____

HOW ARE WE DIFFERENT: _____

_____

_____

ARIES

MODALITY: CARDINAL

DATES: MARCH 21 - APRIL 19

SYMBOL OF ARIES

CONSTELLATION OF ARIES

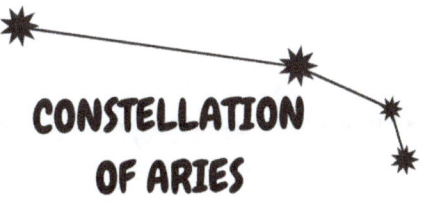

ELEMENT OF ARIES

CHARACTERISTICS

- ENERGETIC
- PASSIONATE
- COMPETITIVE
- NATURAL LEADERS
- IMPULSIVE
- INDEPENDENT
- SOMETIMES ACTS TOO HASTILY
- RECOVER FROM SETBACKS EASILY
- NOT AFRAID TO TRY NEW THINGS
- HAVE A PIONEERING SPIRIT
- INSPIRES OTHERS TO FOLLOW THEIR LEAD

RAM

MY ARIES

HOUSE OF MY ARIES: _____

ARIES I KNOW: _____

HOW ARE WE ALIKE: _____

_____

_____

HOW ARE WE DIFFERENT: _____

_____

_____

LEO

MODALITY: FIXED

DATES: JULY 23 – AUGUST 22

SYMBOL OF LEO

CONSTELLATION OF LEO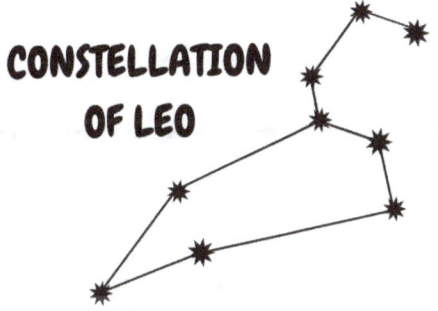

ELEMENT OF LEO

CHARACTERISTICS

LION

- CONFIDENT
- GENEROUS
- THEATRICAL
- NATURAL PERFORMERS
- DEMANDING
- OUTGOING
- COMPETITIVE
- NATURAL LEADER
- CREATIVE
- ENERGETIC
- STYLISH
- PROTECTIVE

MY LEO

HOUSE OF MY LEO: _____

LEOS I KNOW: _____

HOW ARE WE ALIKE: _____

_____

_____

HOW ARE WE DIFFERENT: _____

_____

_____

SAGITTARIUS MODALITY: MUTABLE

DATES: NOVEMBER 22 - DECEMBER 21

SYMBOL OF SAGITTARIUS

CONSTELLATION OF SAGITTARIUS

ELEMENT OF SAGITTARIUS

CHARACTERISTICS

CENTAUR ARCHER

- OPTIMISTIC
- ADVENTUROUS
- INDEPENDENT
- INTELLECTUAL
- HONEST
- IMPULSIVE
- BLUNT
- RESTLESS
- FUNNY
- PHILOSOPHICAL

MY SAGITTARIUS

HOUSE OF MY SAGITTARIUS: _____

SAGITTARIUS' I KNOW: _____

HOW ARE WE ALIKE: _____

_____

_____

HOW ARE WE DIFFERENT: _____

_____

_____

🌍 EARTH SIGNS 🌍

TAURUS, VIRGO, CAPRICORN

People born under the earth element are usually grounded and practical. They are like the soil and rocks that make up the earth – dependable and stable. Earth signs are hardworking and loyal, but they can also be stubborn and resistant to change.

MY EARTH SIGNS

MY EARTH SIGNS: _____

EARTH SIGNS I KNOW: _____

HOW ARE WE ALIKE: _____

_____

_____

HOW ARE WE DIFFERENT: _____

_____

_____

TAURUS

MODALITY: FIXED

DATES: APRIL 20 - MAY 20

SYMBOL OF TAURUS

CONSTELLATION OF TAURUS

ELEMENT OF TAURUS

CHARACTERISTICS

- RELIABLE
- PATIENT
- STUBBORN
- LOYAL
- TRADITIONAL
- GROUNDED
- TRUSTWORTHY
- SENSIBLE
- LOVING
- STABLE

BULL

MY TAURUS

HOUSE OF MY TAURUS: _____

TAURUS' I KNOW: _____

HOW ARE WE ALIKE: _____

_____

_____

HOW ARE WE DIFFERENT: _____

_____

_____

VIRGO

MODALITY: MUTABLE

DATES: AUGUST 23 – SEPTEMBER 22

SYMBOL OF VIRGO

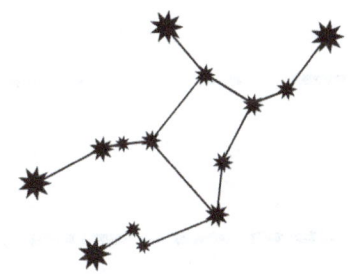

CONSTELLATION OF VIRGO

ELEMENT OF VIRGO

CHARACTERISTICS

VIRGIN MAIDEN

- DETAILED
- THINKER
- ORGANIZED
- MODEST
- RELIABLE
- LOGICAL
- RESERVED
- RESPONSIBLE
- RATIONAL
- HIGH STANDARDS

MY VIRGO

HOUSE OF MY VIRGO: _____

VIRGOS I KNOW: _____

HOW ARE WE ALIKE: _____

_____

_____

HOW ARE WE DIFFERENT: _____

_____

_____

CAPRICORN

MODALITY: CARDINAL

DATES: DECEMBER 22 - JANUARY 19

SYMBOL OF CAPRICORN

CONSTELLATION OF CAPRICORN

ELEMENT OF CAPRICORN

CHARACTERISTICS

- RESPONSIBLE
- AMBITIOUS
- PRACTICLE
- DISCIPLINED
- SERIOUS
- DILIGENT
- TRUSTWORTHY
- WISE
- PATIENT
- ORGANIZED
- SUCCESSFUL

GOAT

MY CAPRICORN

HOUSE OF MY CAPRICORN: _____

CAPRICORNS I KNOW: _____

HOW ARE WE ALIKE: _____

_____

_____

HOW ARE WE DIFFERENT: _____

_____

_____

AIR SIGNS

GEMINI, LIBRA, AQUARIUS

People born under the air element are often very social and curious. They are like the breeze that blows through the trees – always on the move and exploring new ideas. Air signs are communicative and intelligent, but they can also be indecisive and aloof.

MY AIR SIGNS

MY AIR SIGNS: _____

AIR SIGNS I KNOW: _____

HOW ARE WE ALIKE: _____

_____

_____

HOW ARE WE DIFFERENT: _____

_____

_____

GEMINI

MODALITY: MUTABLE

DATES: MAY 21 – JUNE 21

SYMBOL OF GEMINI

CONSTELLATION OF GEMINI

ELEMENT OF GEMINI

CHARACTERISTICS

TWINS

- CURIOUS
- SOCIAL
- ADAPTABLE
- WITTY
- VERSATILE
- TALKATIVE
- EXPRESSIVE
- CREATIVE
- INTELLEGENT
- RESTLESS
- SPONTANEOUS

MY GEMINI

HOUSE OF MY GEMINI: _____

GEMINIS I KNOW: _____

HOW ARE WE ALIKE: _____

_____

_____

HOW ARE WE DIFFERENT: _____

_____

_____

LIBRA

MODALITY: CARDINAL

DATES: SEPTEMBER 23 - OCTOBER 22

SYMBOL OF LIBRA

CONSTELLATION OF LIBRA
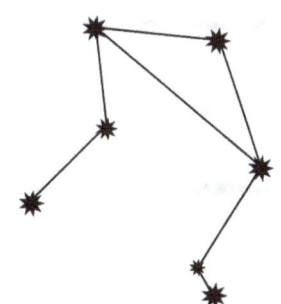

ELEMENT OF LIBRA

CHARACTERISTICS

- FAIR
- CHARMING
- BALANCED
- SOCIABLE
- INDECISIVE
- COOPERATIVE
- IDEALISTIC
- STYLISH
- ARTISTIC
- LOVING

SCALES

MY LIBRA

HOUSE OF MY LIBRA: _____

LIBRAS I KNOW: _____

HOW ARE WE ALIKE: _____

_____

_____

HOW ARE WE DIFFERENT: _____

_____

_____

AQUARIUS

MODALITY: FIXED

DATES: JANUARY 20 - FEBRUARY 18

SYMBOL OF AQUARIUS

CONSTELLATION OF AQUARIUS

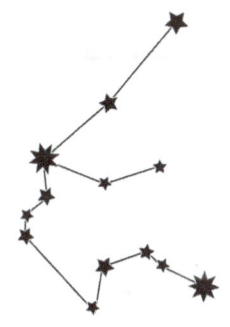

ELEMENT OF AQUARIUS

WATER BEARER

CHARACTERISTICS

- INDEPENDENT
- INTELLECTUAL
- INNOVATIVE
- HELPFUL
- QUIRKY
- UNPREDICTABLE
- FRIENDLY
- VISIONARY
- REBELLIOUS
- ALOOF

MY AQUARIUS

HOUSE OF MY AQUARIUS: _____

AQUARIUS' I KNOW: _____

HOW ARE WE ALIKE: _____

_____

_____

HOW ARE WE DIFFERENT: _____

_____

_____

WATER SIGNS

CANCER, SCORPIO, PISCES

People born under the water element are usually very emotional and intuitive. They are like the waves in the ocean – deep and mysterious. Water signs are empathetic and creative, but they can also be moody and sensitive.

MY WATER SIGNS

MY WATER SIGNS: _____

WATER SIGNS I KNOW: _____

HOW ARE WE ALIKE: _____

_____

_____

HOW ARE WE DIFFERENT: _____

_____

_____

CANCER

MODALITY: CARDINAL

DATES: JUNE 22 - JULY 22

SYMBOL OF CANCER

CONSTELLATION OF CANCER

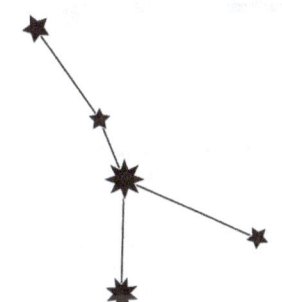

ELEMENT OF CANCER

CHARACTERISTICS

- EMOTIONAL
- NURTURING
- INTUITIVE
- PROTECTIVE
- FAMILIAL
- CREATIVE
- MOODY
- PERSISTENT
- SENTIMENTAL
- COMPASSIONATE

CRAB

MY CANCER

HOUSE OF MY CANCER: _____

CANCERS I KNOW: _____

HOW ARE WE ALIKE: _____

_____

_____

HOW ARE WE DIFFERENT: _____

_____

_____

SCORPIO

MODALITY: FIXED

DATES: OCTOBER 23 - NOBEMBER 21

SYMBOL OF SCORPIO

CONSTELLATION OF SCORPIO

ELEMENT OF SCORPIO

CHARACTERISTICS

- INTENSE
- MYSTERIOUS
- DETERMINED
- RESOURCEFUL
- INDEPENDENT
- PERCEPTIVE
- AMBITIOUS
- COMPLEX
- LOYAL
- POWERFUL

SCORPION

MY SCORPIO

HOUSE OF MY SCORPIO: _____

SCORPIOS I KNOW: _____

HOW ARE WE ALIKE: _____

_____

_____

HOW ARE WE DIFFERENT: _____

_____

_____

PISCES

MODALITY: MUTABLE

DATES: FEBRUARY 19 - MARCH 20

SYMBOL OF PISCES

CONSTELLATION OF PISCES

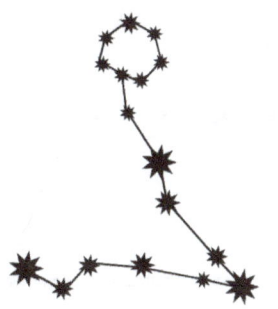

ELEMENT OF PISCES

CHARACTERISTICS

- EMPATHETIC
- INTUITIVE
- CREATIVE
- DREAMY
- COMPASSIONATE
- SENSITIVE
- SPIRITUAL
- DAYDREAMER
- SELFLESS
- GENTLE

TWO FISH

MY PISCES

HOUSE OF MY PISCES: _____

PISCES I KNOW: _____

HOW ARE WE ALIKE: _____

_____

_____

HOW ARE WE DIFFERENT: _____

_____

_____

PLANETS AND ASPECTS COMING SOON!

This book, which is the first in a series of books for beginners in astrology, will set the foundation for your own personalized set of books that contain information from your birth chart. This is just the beginning in creating your own personal astrology guide that will eventually tell your complete story of the "Universe Inside".